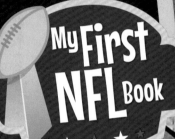

My First NFL Book

PITTSBURGH STEELERS

Nate Cohn

LET'S READ
AV²
BY WEIGL™
ADDED VALUE • AUDIO VISUAL

Go to **www.av2books.com**, and enter this book's unique code.

BOOK CODE

T754252

AV² by Weigl brings you media enhanced books that support active learning.

AV² provides enriched content that supplements and complements this book. Weigl's AV² books strive to create inspired learning and engage young minds in a total learning experience.

Your AV² Media Enhanced books come alive with...

Audio
Listen to sections of the book read aloud.

Video
Watch informative video clips.

Embedded Weblinks
Gain additional information for research.

Try This!
Complete activities and hands-on experiments.

Key Words
Study vocabulary, and complete a matching word activity.

Quizzes
Test your knowledge.

Slide Show
View images and captions, and prepare a presentation.

... and much, much more!

Published by AV² by Weigl
350 5th Avenue, 59th Floor
New York, NY 10118

Website: www.av2books.com

Library of Congress Control Number: 2017930783

ISBN 978-1-4896-5544-8 (hardcover)
ISBN 978-1-4896-5546-2 (multi-user eBook)

Printed in the United States of America in Brainerd, Minnesota
1 2 3 4 5 6 7 8 9 0   21 20 19 18 17

042017
020317

Editor: Katie Gillespie
Art Director: Terry Paulhus

Weigl acknowledges Getty Images, Alamy, and iStock as the primary image suppliers for this title.

My First NFL Book

PITTSBURGH STEELERS

CONTENTS

Team History

Arthur J. Rooney started the Pittsburgh Steelers in 1933. They were called the Pirates then. The team name changed to the Steelers in 1940. This is because Pittsburgh once produced half of the United States' steel.

The Steelers are the only NFL team to win back-to-back Super Bowls twice.

4

The Stadium

The Steelers play at Heinz Field. The stadium's scoreboard has two big ketchup bottles on top. Each one is 35 feet long. Red light pours out of them. Heinz is a Pittsburgh company that makes ketchup and other foods.

Heinz Field is in Pittsburgh, Pennsylvania. It is where three rivers meet.

Team Spirit

A mascot named Steely
McBeam leads the cheering.
Steelers fans spin yellow
towels when they cheer.
The towels were first sold for
a playoff game in 1975. A
radio announcer called them
the "Terrible Towels." They
are still called
by that name.

The money made from
sales of Terrible Towels
goes to charity.

The Jerseys

The Steelers wear black jerseys with yellow stripes. They are the only NFL team to wear black and yellow. These are the official colors of the city of Pittsburgh. The colors are on the city's flag. The city's baseball team also wears these colors.

The Helmet

The Steelers' helmets are black with a yellow stripe. The team's logo is on the right side. The logo is based on the "Steelmark." This is a mark used on items that are made with steel from the United States.

The Steelers are the only NFL team with a logo on just one side of their helmets.

13

14

The Coach

Mike Tomlin is the Steelers' head coach. He had a lot to live up to when he was hired in 2007. The coaches before him were very successful. The team won the Super Bowl in Tomlin's second season. No other Steelers' coach won a title that fast. He was also the youngest NFL coach to ever win the title.

Player Positions

The fullback's job is to run the ball, block for other runners, and catch passes. This player sometimes runs in front of the player with the ball. The fullback pushes tacklers away. This move is called a lead block.

The average time players are in the NFL is 3.5 seasons.

16

Star Player

Le'Veon Bell is a running back. Bell has made his name in the NFL by catching passes. He rushed 167 yards in a 2017 playoff game. That is a team record. Bell went to the Pro Bowl two times in his first four years with the team. This is the yearly game for the best NFL players.

18

"Mean" Joe Greene

was a tackle in the 1970s. He is in the Pro Football Hall of Fame. He got his nickname because he was scary to play against. Greene was part of the "Steel Curtain." That was the name for the Steelers' strong defense. Greene and the Steel Curtain won four Super Bowls.

Famous Player

Team Records

Chuck Noll, Bill Cowher, and Mike Tomlin have been the team's only coaches since 1969. Each one won at least one NFL championship. Noll won four. Only one other NFL coach has won more. The Steelers have won six Super Bowls. That is the most of any NFL team. Placekicker Gary Anderson scored 1,343 points. This is a team record.

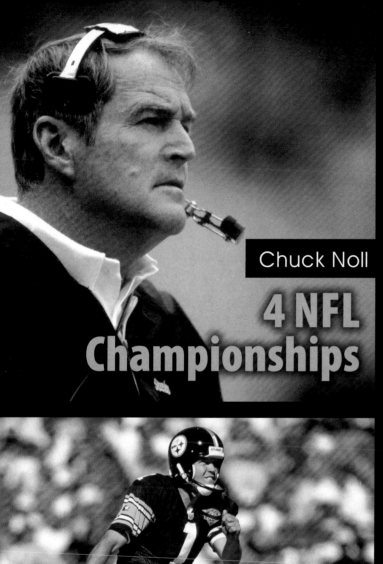

Chuck Noll

4 NFL Championships

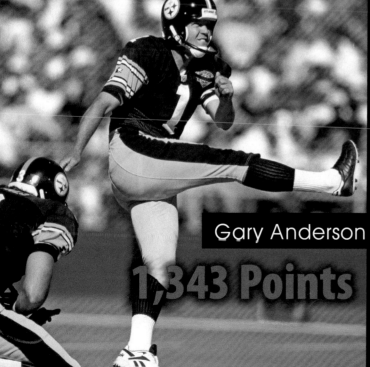

Gary Anderson

1,343 Points

6 Super Bowl Wins

21

By the Numbers

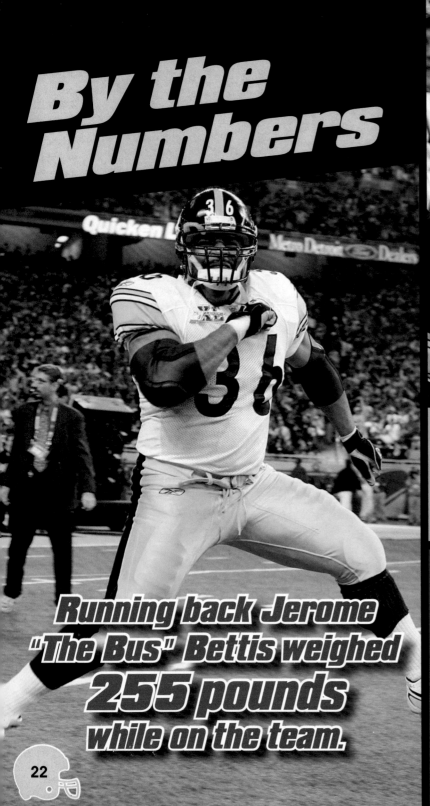

Running back Jerome "The Bus" Bettis weighed 255 pounds while on the team.

Linebacker Jack Lambert made **28 interceptions** in 11 years.

Strong safety Troy Polamalu was named to 8 Pro Bowl teams.

Terrible Towels have raised more than **$3 million** for charity.

Running back Franco Harris rushed more than 1,000 yards in 8 seasons.

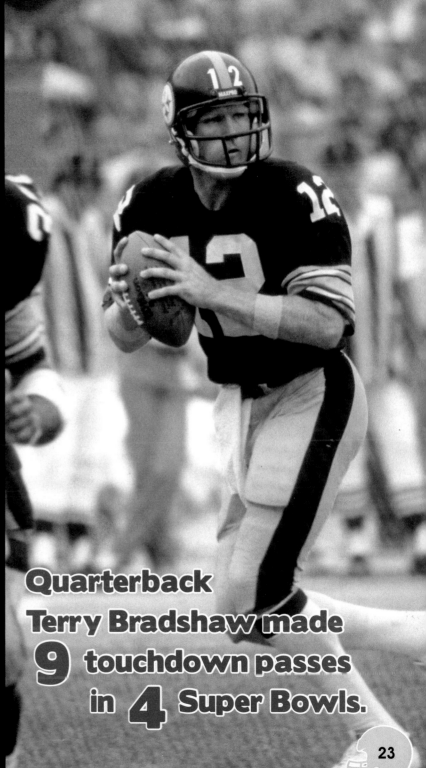

Quarterback Terry Bradshaw made **9** touchdown passes in **4** Super Bowls.

23

Quiz

1. Who founded the Steelers?

2. What is the name of the team's mascot?

3. What was Joe Greene's position on the team?

4. What was the nickname for the Steelers' strong 1970s defense?

5. Which Steelers coach has won the most championships?